PURPOSE IN YOUR PAIN

PURPOSE
IN YOUR PAIN

USING PERSONAL PAIN FOR PROFESSIONAL GAIN

PIPER V. MOORE

Charleston, SC
www.PalmettoPublishing.com

Purpose In Your Pain
Copyright © 2021 by Piper V. Moore

All rights reserved

No portion of this book may be reproduced, stored in a retrieval system, or transmitted in any form by any means—electronic, mechanical, photocopy, recording, or other—except for brief quotations in printed reviews, without prior permission of the author.

First Edition

ISBN: 978-1-68515-564-3

DEDICATION

To Mom,
Thank you for teaching me to disregard the foolish ways of others.
In the words of Grandma Mom,
"Tell them to kiss your ain't in the country
and go about your business."

To my children,
Jacques and Jonti-él, Thank you for helping me find my strength.

To my team of many,
I see through clear lenses and stand on solid ground because of you.

PREFACE

The author, Piper Moore, is an accomplished professional speaker, and a certified executive and personal development coach. She has experienced the benefits of personal breakthroughs through the support of others and the hard lessons of life. In Piper's toolbox you will find determination, discernment, wherewithal, and the refusal to give up in the midst of a storm and festering darkness.

Purpose in Your Pain takes you on a journey through disappointments, setbacks, storms, and the victories of life and career. The message is the teacher, and you will experience your own breakthroughs and learn how to use your personal pain to catapult your professional gain by building upon your intrinsic motivators, strengthening your character, and creating effective behaviors that will become instrumental in your success. The author shares the prominent steps she has taken as she travels her uniquely designed path in life. You will discover how the pains in your life serve a greater purpose than what you can envision in the midst of your darkness and storms.

You are strongest when you believe you are growing weak but refuse to wither. Discover your truth as you embark upon your personal one-on-one coaching session. On this journey you will

1. break down barriers that you have unconsciously concealed,
2. identify your strengths that evolved from your experiences, and
3. understand the purpose of your pain.

Without a say in the matter, everyone must travel their own journey through life. A journey that is independent of the journeys of those who contribute to your life. This life is uniquely designed for you to thrive.

TABLE OF CONTENTS

Prologue	xi
Chapter 1: Trying to Understand	1
Chapter 2: Giving Life to Desires	4
Chapter 3: Recognizing Prosperity	7
Chapter 4: Soaring with a Team	10
Chapter 5: Winning with Blinders On	17
Chapter 6: Build That Fortress	22
Chapter 7: Gearing *Up*	25
Chapter 8: The Purpose	29
Epilogue	34
Psalm 27: King James Version (KJV)	36
About the Author	38

PROLOGUE

I never understood the hate, the hurt, or the turmoil that others persistently and diligently brought into my life. I still struggle in comprehending how so many people do their best work in dark places to the point of self-destruction while trying to hurt me. Their behaviors remind me of the chorus in Gerald Levert's song "Point the Finger," which says when you point your finger at someone, there are three fingers pointing back at you. Yes, I tested this theory, and it is true. I pointed one finger forward, looked at my hand, and there were three fingers pointing directly at me. I interpreted this to say that no one can speak of someone else's flaws, experiences, or choices without first assessing their own. Contrary to the beliefs of some, in the eyes of others, everyone has a flaw or two. The song continues on to say that the accusation someone is making is probably something the person who is pointing the finger would do. Of course, I am paraphrasing the lyrics. This made me reconsider how much attention and energy I should expend on others' negative actions and their interpretation of who I am based upon the person they desire me to be.

It wasn't until I realized I loved myself that the wicked ways of others had no power over my life. This was a pivotal moment for me because it is when I recognized the inner strength that was developing with every step forward I took in the many valleys where I was forced to walk and where I refused to lie down. At the time, I did not know how to reference what was going on inside of me, but I knew it was change and I liked the way it felt. I realized what I was feeling was embedded in my spirit before I entered this world. The purpose of its existence was to guide my navigation beyond the negative feelings I once had because of the many downturns of my life and how I was treated by others.

The moment I realized that the hell others had tried to put me through was just a warm breeze passing by and not a permanent tropical storm. I was able to smile and fight past the dark times of life. Enduring and withstanding the behaviors that were charging toward me at top speed made my skin tough, my back strong, my eyes open, and my mind wise. Yes, it even gave my voice power.

What I know now is that I was completely oblivious during the years true dislike was being dispensed in my direction. In part because I want to believe that everyone is kind, and their behaviors were unintentional. I was also unaware of my own strengths and the fact that I cannot make everyone comfortable with my journey. Nor was I given an extension on my twenty-four hours each day to designate time to trying to figure out why people carried the emotions that they toted around like expensive luggage. If I knew back then what I know now, I would not be the woman who I am today. So praise God that some things were kept a secret until I was equipped to receive the truth and be accepting of my journey. This pain is called *wisdom*.

Wisdom brings forth insurmountable discernment. Obedience to discernment has exposed forthcoming harm and allowed me to prepare my protection. It has allowed me to be a conduit that delivers a message of encouragement at the right time for the right person. Because I learned to listen to the spirit of discernment and love myself, I am equipped to support others as they move beyond their fears and witness the gratitude on the other side of the fear.

Nothing you go through is for naught. Are you listening with opened eyes? Every emotional, psychological, and yes, even some physical pain that you have endured has purpose. It is time for you discover the *Purpose in Your Pain*.

CHAPTER 1

Trying to Understand

They, devout religious and spiritual beings, say that the Lord will not give you more than you can bear. I have had many times in my life where I have questioned whether or not there was any conceivable truth in that old, familiar cliché. Even though I questioned it, I wanted to believe that the words they spoke were a truth I would soon discover. All my life I was told that I had a twin, someone who looks just like me, she also resided in Middletown, Ohio, and her name was Tammy. I often wondered if God had mistaken me for Tammy and given me all of her problems. I was truly trying to understand.

Living life takes intentional efforts, but existing only requires waking up. I have learned that I have choices and I am empowered to choose what I want to achieve and some of the experiences that I desire while living this life fully. It is mine, so I have decided not to assist anyone in being delusional in believing that they can choose the direction of my life or my happiness for me. However, years one through eighteen and six months were the exceptions.

I grew up the eldest of two children in a single-parent home with my mother. My parents divorced when I was five years old, and my sister was two years old. My memory has very little recollection of what it feels like to live in a two-parent home. Even after the divorce, we still spent some time with Daddy. It wasn't consistent, but it was time. He later remarried, and I became the eldest of three children.

My family, in this regard, functioned like most multi-generational families. I grew up at my maternal grandparents' house. That was where all of us grandkids spent our time while our parents worked or were partaking in their leisure time. In order of age with the grandchildren, I fell right in the middle. I spent more time with my grandmother than any other grandchild. I had a lot of overnight sleepovers with my grandmother, whom I call Mom. She introduced me to road trips as I traveled to Tennessee with her and her posse of cousins and friends. Growing up, I enjoyed my time with Mom. Because of my enjoyment, I did not try to understand why out of almost fifteen (now twenty-two) grandchildren, I spent the most time with my grandmother. Mom often took me to work with her. We still laugh when she tells the story of how I proudly wore my knitted hat in the summertime that she had knitted for me to wear on cold winter days. Mrs. Martin, Mom's employer, tried to get me to take my hat off because I was sweating profusely. I refused because Mom told me that I should always wear a hat to keep my head warm, and besides, Mom knitted that hat just for me.

My ability to stand alone and stand out began in my primitive years. Maybe this is where the term *black sheep* was birthed. Being under Mom's tutelage, I learned how to cook and crochet well. I even became a regular attendee at the bingo hall until they implemented an over-twelve rule. For a while, I continued to go to bingo with Mom, though I was not quite twelve; I believe I was around nine. Mom dared anyone to say something to her about my age or my attendance. Yep, that is the strong tree from whence I come. I do recall there being a very short period of time when I was unable to go to bingo because of the rule, but somehow, I ended up right back in the hall with my grandma and my own bingo cards.

I was always inquisitive but too shy or simply too damaged to ask questions. I often hid my true feelings deep in the pit of my stomach until they would dissipate. I would simply go as told and sometimes force a smile as I moved in the assigned direction. I was ecstatic about learning new things, especially when it came to cooking, because of Mom. She would not ask if I wanted to learn; she would simply bring me next to her and show me.

As the years passed, something rose inside of me, and I wanted more in life. At that time, I could not identify what the feeling was. Later in my teenage years, I defined this feeling as my drive to achieve professional success beyond what I had seen in my family. I had no direction on what to do with this feeling, mainly because I didn't know how to communicate what I was experiencing or who to share it with, so I just tried to understand.

What part of your life are you trying to understand?

_____
_____
_____
_____
_____
_____
_____
_____
_____

MEDITATE.

CHAPTER 2

Giving Life to Desires

I have found it very interesting to recognize how feelings transitioned my growth as time passed by, even when I did not fully understand. I know that I am not alone in this experience, but my experience is different than any other being simply because it is mine. Yes, it is called self-awareness for a reason. No one knew how I felt. Heck, I am not sure anyone was remotely concerned or even interested in how I felt. At this moment, no one else mattered. No one could tell me how I was supposed to feel. Nor was I obligated to share what I was feeling in a manner that would make others comfortable. Oh yes, I was growing in me, and emotions are *real*. I felt like I was that flower on the verge of blooming. The seed was planted by God, watered by life, and destined to flourish.

Bloom, baby, bloom—words I have learned to speak to myself. The more I listened to the desires within my spirit, the more I knew it was up to me to give them life. Not only did I desire a career, I also wanted to purchase a house and complete a college degree, which had not been achieved in my family. I enjoyed my family, but I always knew I was different. Sometimes being different was rewarded by a large dose of pain. Through this pain I learned that I cannot expect people to support what they do not understand or what they have not successfully achieved themselves. This pain was called *reality check*.

I really love bringing people together, and as a family we always had a great time. Birthdays are very important to me, so I made it a priority to wish everyone a happy birthday if I was aware of their special day. I initiated adult family dinners for birthday celebrations, and my family received it well. We celebrated this for a few years. Though I attended solo, as the only single person in the family, I had a great time, again because we were celebrating someone's special day. Soon after I began giving life to my desires, all that shifted into a different direction. It is interesting how people change when you begin to prosper, as they see it. Birthday dinners started happening without me. I guess another way of stating it is by saying point-blank I was no longer invited. This began after I purchased my first home. Yes, this was a new pain. One that was intentionally afflicted upon me.

Someone once said that there is nothing like family. I surely hope the author of that quote is correct—sheesh. Yes, it did hurt, and all I did was be myself. Authentically and unapologetically me. During this time period, my children stopped receiving invitations to family birthday parties and a couple sleepovers for the children of the adults who shunned me. I am so glad that there is nothing like family. Believing this gave me hope for brighter and happier days.

Here comes more pain when I must explain to my children, who are now saddened, why they were not invited to their cousins' parties or sleepovers. My pain immediately shifted to anger. When someone wrongs or outright mistreats my children, I put my heart on ice. I refocused to look at what really mattered, and less focus was given to what did not deserve my attention or my time. Once I made the conscious decision to focus on what mattered, I was then able to get my heart and mind to communicate. I cannot change family. I did not ask for them; they were gifted to me. So be it. I have to provide a good life for my children and pursue the desires of my heart. I am all that we have, and my children will be survivors, destined for greatness.

Time to pursue my education. I wonder how family will change now. Truthfully, I ran out of time to care. So family, thank you for the pain that ignited the inferno that fueled my desires and propelled me into prosperity. My desires now have life. This pain is called *strength*.

What has pain buried inside of you that needs to be given life?

_____
_____
_____
_____
_____
_____
_____

Step 1: Release the pain.
Speak aloud (three times):
At this moment, I release _____
_____
I no longer give it power in my life.

Step 2:_____
_____

MEDITATE.

CHAPTER 3

Recognizing Prosperity

Freedom really feels great! Being free from the unnecessary cares and evils of the world has given me clear lenses. I see happiness, I see vision, I see opportunities for my life, I see my possibilities.

The fact that I no longer expend energy or thought on the negativity of others has rejuvenated my power and advanced my drive to succeed at everything in life. Sometimes I sit back and smile because the pain from life and the pain that was intentionally afflicted on me and my children has help me love myself. I am emotionally stronger and wiser. The pain has given me the extra push that I needed to put my plan for professional prosperity into action. The Bible states in Genesis 50:20 that what man meant for evil God uses for good. There is purpose in my pain. This pain is called *rise*.

I define prosperity as purposeful growth. Through my many years of peaks and valleys, I discovered that prosperity does not occur solely in the professional realm. I think my personal prosperity exceeds my grandest vision of my professional prosperity. Yet it is because of my personal growth that I have a solid foundation to stand on professionally. See, what I know is that I am one person, not divided by professionalism, and I am uniquely me. One who is trying, with everything I have, to be professionally successful. To stand in who I want to be as I develop into who I am going to be.

That was my life for twenty-five years. I finally realized that I was prematurely depositing energy into the wrong areas of my life. I can see now that it was a way to escape my past while I continue to reach for my future. What I believe to be truth is that I should have escaped my past by addressing it, understanding it, and growing from it twenty years ago. Achieving such a large feat would have allowed me to be myself completely, personally, and professionally, confident in both. This awakening moment began my season for prosperity, and this just scratched the surface. I know this to be factual because I have grown emotionally, advanced my education, practiced self-love, and have professional direction. If I were ever asked the question, "What does prosperity look like to me?" I would gladly reply, "Prosperity looks like living in your truth when your truth was once buried by pain, hatred, and low confidence—*unapologetically*."

Reflect on your past pains and the person you are today. In what part of your life have you experienced the greatest growth?

_____
_____
_____
_____
_____
_____
_____

MEDITATE.

Now, celebrate your growth!

CHAPTER 4

Soaring with a Team

In life we all have our own personalized paths to travel, by God's design. We do not know where, when, or how our paths will end or the number of curves we will face as we travel through our journey. Often, we step gingerly, one foot in front of the other, one day at a time. When life is going in our desired direction and the path is colored gold, our steps tend to be bold, and our confidence is strong. I learned that even when the path becomes cloudy and dusted with darkness, the bold and confident strides should pummel the path. Fear can immobilize you and deplete your confidence, softening your stride. Stepping boldly and confidently signals to fear that it has no place on your path.

My journey has been the epitome of a solo trip. It was not until my early thirties that I witnessed people joining me on my journey as an adult. Up to this point, there were individuals who served as untitled mentors in my life. What they instilled in me remains a part of me today. The ability to recognize opportunity and decipher if it is a beneficial opportunity for me did not come easily. I am quite sure that I am not alone in my eagerness to secure every opportunity that is placed in front me. Yet I have learned that though I may be presented with what appears to be a great opportunity, if it does not propel me closer to my goal and align with the steps I must take to achieve any goal that I have established, it may be a great opportunity for someone else. It can be challenging to walk away from such an opportunity, yet I have learned that accepting opportunities best suited for someone else can exhaust time and energy that I should apply toward my action steps to achieve my goal. I believe it is best practice to always exercise kindness through showing of appreciation when I am presented with opportunities that I cannot accept.

It appears to me that every phase of life begins a new part of my journey. The more years of life I am blessed with, the more significant my journey becomes. There are grander responsibilities as an adult than one could fathom as a teenager. Some things I asked for in my early adult years, I did not receive, like the big corporate job with the great company and six-figure salary, where I was required to work in a suit and carry a briefcase. Some things I did not ask for but did receive, like being on my own at age eighteen, the official age of becoming an adult, and a single parent by the age of nineteen. When I realized that others were joining me on my journey, I interpreted this action as God's way of affirming that I do not walk alone.

Everyone who I needed was sent into my life at the time when I needed them most, often for a purpose unbeknownst to me. Because of the craziness of my journey, I could not fathom the difference strangers could make in my life. Yes, I understood how I had begun to positively impact the lives of others, but rarely had I experienced someone positively impacting mine.

What I witnessed through experience caused me to welcome everyone who joined me on my journey even without knowing if they entered my life for a reason, a season, or a lifetime. I learned to be accepting of the purpose they were sent to serve without trying to change their purpose to suit what I felt was my greatest need at that moment. The people in my life brought me out of my darkness into my new beginning.

Darkness had created a coating over my eyes and my heart. So, when I opened my mouth to speak, I verbalized my dark emotions and thoughts. During this period of my life, I worked for a local government organization. While attending a community event for the organization, supporting the local United Way chapter, I was reacquainted with Melissa. Melissa was someone whom I vaguely knew from primary school. We lived in a small town, Middletown, Ohio, and even though we did not interact, we had mutual friends and knew each other by name. Needless to say, we were not complete strangers, but we did become acquaintances. Again, not knowing if she was entering my life for a reason, a season, or a lifetime or if she was filling a need that I was oblivious to, I welcomed getting to know her.

Melissa and I shared many commonalities. We were both active in our organizations and the community, single parents, supportive, and God-fearing women. There was always value in our conversations. I must say that I am very pleased with myself for not trying to figure out why we met. Our relationship has evolved over the years to where she is no longer an acquaintance; she is my friend.

There are so many facets in life where we need the company of others to hold ourselves accountable. After many conversations about improving our health and energy levels, Melissa and I agreed to increase our cardio activity to improve our overall health. In an effort to support one another, we scheduled days and times to walk together in the evenings after work. This commitment that we made to one another improved more than our daily cardio. Exercise stimulated our endorphins, which decreased our stress and tension, garnering greater improvement than what we sought out to achieve. I must not forget to mention the significant improvement in sleep that we both reported. It also increased our oxygen flow to the brain, supporting healthy cognitive behavior that resulted in better focus and mental clarity. All of this from the simple act of walking. How do I know that walking did all of this, you ask? Because I understand my body's language and how great I felt. I slept better, and my thoughts were clear.

For Melissa and me, walking was an opportunity for us to talk about anything and everything. You know, we had the good, no-holds-barred, anything-goes conversations. There was one particular day that has replayed in my mind like it was yesterday. The weather was calm, and it was a beautiful late-summer evening around 6:00 p.m., which was our normal walking time. I recall a moment in our conversation where I was talking and she was actively listening. When I finished speaking, I looked at her in a way that my eyes were saying, "You know what I mean?" In return, I awaited her "Yes, I do" look or a couple of head nods in agreement. Instead, I was given that "My goodness, you are miserable" look. Her look expressed exactly how I was feeling.

I reflected on that experience over the next couple of days. During my reflection time, I discovered that misery does not feel good. I did not like how it felt, and I had to do something to change my life. I know that I was destined for so much more in life. I knew I deserved to be happy.

During this time, my son was in his senior year of high school, and my daughter had just entered her freshman year in high school. I knew that identifying what I needed to do was not something I could do alone. I was not in a stable, peaceful emotional state. Past experiences taught me that making emotional decisions were counterproductive for me. I turned to God for direction on my next step. My direction was not revealed immediately. In fact, it took nearly nine months.

During this waiting period, in April 2009, my daughter and I visited Marietta, Georgia. Living in Georgia had been a desire in my heart for many years. My life as a mother was priority over my personal desires. All my decisions had to be made with my children's best interest at the forefront. So, it was imperative that we visit areas around the best schools in Marietta because her education was, and still is, important to me. Marietta had the top-ranked high schools in Cobb County—Pope High and Sprayberry High. Both schools were located in thriving communities with the convenience of amenities and restaurants. Cobb County was a place I believed we could make our home. To that, should we decide to relocate, the "where" factor was now obsolete.

The purpose for our visit was to determine if then was the right time for us to change our home state from Ohio to Georgia. What I did not realize until after our visit to Georgia was that a portion of my unhappiness was not wanting to live in my small town anymore. Though I had come to this realization, I was unable to determine what specifics about my small town I no longer wanted to be a part of. Maybe it was simply that I had outgrown it. This pain is called *uncertainty*.

We did eventually move to Georgia in August 2009. Living in Georgia affected my life in ways that I never would have imagined. Coming from the northern state of Ohio, my daughter and I experienced the south, individually and collectively, in ways that we could not have preconceived. Even if someone had told me so, I would not have believed in my life that I would have experienced the tapestry of great pleasure and great pain all during the same season of life, some of which almost destroyed me. Yes, Georgia has a story—at least a chapter—to be told and in my forthcoming book *In This Life*," it shall be told.

My friend James, who I met through work several years prior to relocating to Georgia, was a great supporter and motivator in the next phase of my journey. He is a testament to the fact that we never know who will be in our lives for a lifetime nor where or when we will need them most. Nor do we know the need they will fulfill in our lives. This is in part because the "why" appears as time passes by and the relationship grows. It is hard to project what our future needs will be, and often it is a challenge to identify our present needs. Therefore, it is important to keep moving forward and upward even when you are uncertain and feel that you are moving alone. Our life stories have been written; we just have to show up for the rehearsals and bring our A-game at showtime.

Just before leaving Middletown, James gifted me with a DVD of *Beyond the Secret*. Nearly ten years later, I will occasionally pop it in as a reminder that life is a journey full of experiences. A reminder to myself to keep moving forward and upward. I learned that the depth of a relationship determines the title given to those in the relationship. Much the same as going from friend to girlfriend to wife. It is as simple as deciding when you call someone friend or acquaintance and how a friend becomes family. I am appreciative of all of my relationships, good and less than desired, because they helped to mold me into the marvelous person that I am today.

My relationship with Leigha, whom I have known all my life, grew significantly as adults. Over the years, her title changed from *family* to family and friend. She was my motivator and my cheerleader on this journey. She covered me in prayer and lent me her ear even when I felt like life was falling apart and I could not comprehend the *how* or *why* behind the destruction. I came to realize that some things God will only reveal after I have completed the test. My greatest takeaway from my experience with relationships is the recognition that I need them.

On your journey, you will not travel alone. Recognize your team. List the five key players on your team and the role each has in your life.

_____
_____
_____
_____
_____
_____
_____
_____
_____
_____

EXPRESS GRATITUDE

In detail, outline how each person on your team can support your next step.

CHAPTER 5

Winning with Blinders On

One thing that is for certain is in every game, including life, the players change and often shift from team to team. I must admit that I have had times when I was the only player on my team. The forward was *me*; the point guard was *me*; the coach—well, that was me too. There were other times when I had a strong team of more than twenty players. When you find yourself in this game of pain, purpose, and prosperity, you have to understand that it is up to you to know which players make it to the starting lineup and who needs to hold down the bench, metaphorically speaking.

Subconsciously, I have found myself pressing forward while I was spinning in the funnel of a tornado. Often my children were the force behind me that was propelling me forward. I realized that if I became stagnant or stuck in my pain, my children would be stuck with me. My mindset was that I was my children's everything. I was all that they had. I must provide for their every need from the kiss on the forehead as I tucked them into bed, their voice when only their eyes are speaking and their comforter in the emergency room. Being present with thoughts of my children's well-being running through my mind, I had no other choice but to thrive in my job.

My children and I had needs, and their needs required money. I needed my job in order to earn money to provide for our basic needs as well the things we desired. I did not have anyone to call upon for financial assistance, so my only option was to excel, and that is exactly what I did. After the proverbial quitting bell rang at work, I still sought out opportunities to broaden my knowledge and our experiences. We enjoyed frequently traveling outside of Middletown. Traveling was the method I used to expose my children to the beauty of the world and new experiences. We would also spend time reading at the library, watching movies together, visiting new restaurants, and being involved in the community. Everything came with a cost. Even the free events required gas in the car, parking was at a cost, and we needed money for snacks. Again, even free events came at a cost.

But when the night sky engulfed my home and my children were resting, I was thrust back into the eye of the tornado. I prayed, Lord, thank you for another day, for my children, a strong mind, and a kind heart. Lord, please easy my pain. I am tired of struggling. I appreciate the ability to work, but why can't I be compensated for the work that I actually do? Why can't I have the opportunities that seem to come so easily to my coworkers? Lord, I'm tired of hunger pangs but grateful that I can feed my children creative dishes and they never know my struggle. For every day I was blessed to wake and have a job to go to, I simply said thank you. Looking at my children put a smile on my face and prepared me to give 120 percent at work, even when I was subjected to a less than desired environment.

Throughout my career I have been in several environments where the individual whom I reported to directly did not like me and made it known. But God! I had inner peace, but I am human and, yes, at times their behaviors toward me cause my emotions to rise. During these periods in my life, I was unaware of how to be emotionally intelligent and still maintain control. I had to feed my babies. Often, I felt angry, frustrated, irritated, and downright pissed. No matter how I felt, I did not allow my quality of work to diminish. I was persistent with making recommendations for improvement within the organization and my core group. The recommendations that I made were for changes that I knew I could make. I was willing to roll up my sleeves and get my hands dirty in effort to complete the task in addition to maintaining the workload for which I was already responsible. I created growth opportunities for myself that garnered recognition of my skills and talents. I would also volunteer when I was able to. If my volunteer opportunities were community-based events, my children and I volunteered as a family.

Hindsight is always twenty-twenty, at least that is the old adage I had always heard. I often found myself reflecting on past achievements. As I looked back at every position I held and my involvement during my tenure, I took pride in my goal to always leave my mark in the organization. The mark I made was also focused on organizational improvement that benefited the organization, employees, and the community in some facet. I have been laid off from work many times. Some of the companies where I experienced the lay-off were companies that I made notable improvements for. Not long after my employment with the organization expired, I had to ask myself—why? Why did I give so much to so many who would not pay me my worth? Even beyond my job, I would ask myself why I gave so much to so many who would not do the same for me.

As I reflect back, I believe my strong work ethic was stimulated by my desire to mask my pain. So in return, my pain produced promotions, degrees, certifications, and accomplishments that are not printed on paper. Reflecting is the value of what aligns you to your present and steers you into your next.

What have you given that significantly benefited someone else?

_____
_____
_____

What did you give?

_____
_____
_____

Why did you give it?

_____
_____
_____

Will you do it again?

_____
_____
_____

What is the benefit to you for doing or not doing it again?

_____
_____
_____

How will you use this benefit to win?

_____
_____
_____

Continue writing your thoughts or words of emotional expression.

CHAPTER 6

Build That Fortress

Everything has purpose. Yes, even your pain. Much like building a brick house, with every layer you become stronger, your foundation becomes sound, and your "how" is clearly defined. When the first brick is laid, it stands alone, positioned for what may come next. Alone, it can still be moved to the left, to the right, forward, and backward. If a strong, swift force makes an impact against the brick, it can easily be uprooted and moved into a space where it does not belong.

When a second brick is strategically laid to the right, adjacent to the first brick, and another one to the left and one more directly on top, the first brick becomes immovable. You are that brick that once stood alone. You are becoming what life has created you to be. Be powerful in all that you are.

Throughout my journey, each brick laid represented another layer of my growing strength and my empowerment. For every wind, rain, and hailstorm that raged up against me, it made me stronger because I refused to allow the storm to permeate my spirit. My skin was my protector, and everything flowed downward until it was under my feet. I was built to deflect the storms. I had been molded by life to withstand pain without giving it permission to harm me. I was built to deflect it (Psalms 18:39). Now I can see a future. Now I purposely pursue opportunity that aligns with all that I am, who I am, and who I desire to be. I have built my fortress, and that fortress I call *me*. I am a product of my pain. My strength and my wisdom are biproducts of my suffering. Finding me was the purpose of my pain.

What is the truth on which you stand?

_____
_____
_____
_____
_____
_____
_____
_____

Who are you?

_____
_____
_____
_____
_____
_____
_____
_____

Be grateful for your pain.
Let your scars show. Someone needs to see your scars to believe that they can grow.

Celebrate your victories.
Be your own cheerleader. You played the game and won.

Walk in your purpose.
Never forget where you once were. Put your attention and focus on where you are and how far you have traveled. Keep your eyes planted on where you are going. Take your strength, confidence, and power into your career—the one you have chosen, not one you that you settle for. Get out of your career what you put into it just as you did when you were building your fortress.

CHAPTER 7

Gearing *Up*

Ready or not, with awareness comes responsibility. I know that the desire of many was not solely that I not succeed but that I fail miserably. See, what I know is people. When inner peace is absent and their lives lack true fulfillment—because of the lenses through which they view themselves, or the drive they lack and wish they had, or the fact that they have not been acquainted with self-love—they are comfortable when others are equally unfulfilled.

I have come to realize that sometimes it is as simple as they wish they could be more like me. Able to withstand the storm. Able to smile through hatred. Able to live according to the desires of my heart and not conform to the choices of those around me. Able to travel my path and through it all, able to *love myself* unconditionally and to be myself unapologetically.

My journey, thus far, has taught me how to accept the good in life and the less desirables of life. I have learned to accept what is for me, without doubting, because I am worthy of all the blessings. I am worthy of all the wealth. I am worthy of fulfillment. I am worthy to be happy. I am worthy to have my heart overflow with joy. I am worthy of letting my light shine. I am worthy to be used to help others find purpose in their pain. I should maintain my standards, and I should not settle for less than I deserve, which I have done more times than I care to admit. I deserve the best of all things, and that is exactly what I have received.

What will you do to be ready for
your next chapter in life?

_____
_____
_____
_____
_____
_____

What do you need to set free to
prepare for your best life?

_____
_____
_____
_____
_____
_____

GEAR UP!

EIGHT PRINCIPLES FOR FINDING THE PURPOSE IN YOUR PAIN

1. Live in your truth!
2. Be cognizant of the emotions your pain ignites.
3. Decide to control your emotions and not allow your emotions to control your actions.
4. Pursue three goals that procrastination, due to pain, has kept unfulfilled.
5. Do not overthink the situation or the process but accept reality.
6. Acknowledge what you will no longer accept.
7. Be strong, unapologetic, and consistent in your actions.
8. Recognize what your pain is controlling.

BONUS PRINCIPLE:

1. Commit to personal development coaching to remove barriers created by your pain that are delaying your success.

Your thoughts:

_____
_____
_____
_____
_____
_____
_____
_____

Your commitment:

_____
_____
_____
_____
_____
_____
_____
_____
_____

CHAPTER 8

The Purpose

If it were not for my pain, I would not be the person I am today: driven, confident, and accomplished in my own right. Thank you to all who contributed. It is not the path I would have chosen if I were given the option to choose my journey and the intricacies thereof. Yet because I was not able to choose, the purpose of my journey was manifesting with every forward step that I took, regardless of how heavy my legs were, how sore my back was, or how deep my healing wounds were. What mattered is that I persevered. Through my lenses I saw and still see life as an opportunity. Because God felt that I was deserving of another day, I had work to complete, experiences to enjoy, memories to make, and lives to impact.

As a child I lived with my mother, then with my father, again with my mother, back to Daddy's, and one more return to Mama's house. This was all preparation for my walk into my purpose. At age eighteen, I was put out of my mother's home with my personal belongings and whatever I had in my head and my heart. I was used to going from home to home, so this period in my life was not a difficult adjustment for me. My greatest challenge was determining where I was going to lay my head from night to night. Thank God for my Aunt Deadaux and my maternal grandparents, who willingly assumed the role of parents. I affectionately call them Mom and Dad.

When I was a child, my grandparents resided in the same home, and this is where I spent most of my time. By the time that I was a teenager, they had separated. So, at the beginning of my pregnancy at the age of eighteen, I moved in with Mom. In my final trimester, I lived with Dad, and Dad's house was my son's first home. They helped me at no charge. Because I was put out of my mother's home, I learned to be resourceful and how to take care of myself as an adult. At the arrival of my son, my firstborn child, I was nineteen, and I was not clueless on surviving life. I knew what a child needed. I knew what I needed. I knew of many available resources, and I knew we needed a home. What I did not know, but I learned when my son was two weeks old, was the deadly power of spinal meningitis. Let me recap that: age nineteen, living in temporary housing, new to motherhood, single parent, and my two-week-old child had been stricken with spinal meningitis.

I believe taking on these challenges increased my business acumen and personal presentation. In the service industry, I learned quickly that people tend to treat you better if you are knowledgeable and speak professionally. You know, be their equal. I did my best with my appearance because poor is real. Some say it is a state of mind, but when your living expenses are twice as much as your income, you have a true deficit. It is in this moment poor is not a state of mind; it is a tangible reality. It is also reality that appearance plays a part in how some people choose to treat you. It is unfortunate, but it is reality.

Now I represented myself and my son. Growing into this professional, well-presented being, helped me to secure professional positions throughout my career. I have held positions an executive assistant, trainer, project manager, and receptionist. In many of my positions, I was the first person in my department who internal and external customers engaged with, equally within my organization. I set the tone for their business experience.

In my career, I witnessed people who far exceeded my level of professional achievements, which positioned them to also surpass me in lifestyle quality. They drove nicer cars and could afford good car insurance. Most of them were homeowners and were still in position to buy food and take vacations. I wanted that life. I learned to ask questions and to take interest in learning about the journey of others because this is how I discovered their "how and why." How they were able to achieve what I viewed as success. What was their driving force, and what kept them motivated? The reason or reasons behind why they kept striving from more and succeeding in what they set out to achieve, id est, their defined goals. This fueled my drive to achieve greater heights professionally. My children and I deserved to experience this world through vacations and new experiences and to have the ability to eat in the process and have car insurance. I can honestly say that I did not receive everything that I sought after, but I believe wholeheartedly that I received everything that was meant for me in that moment.

As I advanced professionally, I discovered that I had a gift for helping others find their truth, discover their strengths, and break down barriers. Because the city manager, my director, and my peers all believed in me and I was given opportunities that none of my predecessors had pursued, lo and behold, the facilitator and the speaker in me were released. It took others to bring to my attention my gift of speaking. Once I was made aware of my gift, through the acknowledgement of others and the results of my actions, I consciously set aside a sufficient amount of time to view recordings of my presentations. I needed to witness for myself what others were experiencing through me. Upon viewing my recordings and hearing the power and passion in my voice, I was engulfed with the desire to be so much more by using my gifts (i.e., *purpose*).

Understanding my gift to communicate, I began writing poetry more frequently and with purpose. The interesting fact about me and poetry is that I cannot write because I made a conscious decision to write but because I learned to write when the words are laid in my spirit and are ready to be birthed. I can recall so many mornings that I was awaken at 3:00 a.m. with a poem to write. I learned to keep a pad of paper and an ink pen next to my bed. It is easier, so much easier, to go back to sleep when I never get out the bed and all I have to do is write and roll over. This is a lesson that I learned quickly. My communication skills, my passion to help others, my poetry, my pain, this book, my *purpose*.

As a child, what was your deepest pain?
_____
_____
_____
_____
_____

Are you unconsciously inflicting this same pain onto someone else?
_____
_____
_____
_____
_____

Truth—in what way have you inflicted this same pain onto others? (Your children, spouse, coworkers, etc.)

_____
_____
_____
_____
_____
_____
_____

How has this pain impacted your relationships?

_____
_____
_____
_____
_____
_____
_____

How do you feel about yourself today?

_____
_____
_____
_____
_____
_____
_____

EPILOGUE

Your life's experiences have the propensity to build the muscles of resiliency, awareness, self-love, assertiveness, and forward-thinking. The lenses through which you view your experiences will determine how you will apply what you have learned and how your experiences will manifest in your life. You have the autonomy to choose.

ALWAYS SEEK TO FIND…*PURPOSE IN YOUR PAIN.*

Dear God, thank you for choosing me. Love,

_____

Purpose in Your Pain

PSALM 27
KING JAMES VERSION (KJV)

27 The Lord is my light and my salvation; whom shall I fear? the Lord is the strength of my life; of whom shall I be afraid?

²When the wicked, even mine enemies and my foes, came upon me to eat up my flesh, they stumbled and fell.

³Though an host should encamp against me, my heart shall not fear: though war should rise against me, in this will I be confident.

⁴One thing have I desired of the Lord, that will I seek after; that I may dwell in the house of the Lord all the days of my life, to behold the beauty of the Lord, and to enquire in his temple.

⁵For in the time of trouble he shall hide me in his pavilion: in the secret of his tabernacle shall he hide me; he shall set me up upon a rock.

⁶And now shall mine head be lifted up above mine enemies round about me: therefore, will I offer in his tabernacle sacrifices of joy; I will sing, yea, I will sing praises unto the Lord.

⁷Hear, O Lord, when I cry with my voice: have mercy also upon me and answer me.

⁸ When thou saidst, Seek ye my face; my heart said unto thee, Thy face, Lord, will I seek.

⁹ Hide not thy face far from me; put not thy servant away in anger: thou hast been my help; leave me not, neither forsake me, O God of my salvation.

¹⁰ When my father and my mother forsake me, then the Lord will take me up.

¹¹ Teach me thy way, O Lord, and lead me in a plain path, because of mine enemies.

¹² Deliver me not over unto the will of mine enemies: for false witnesses are risen up against me, and such as breathe out cruelty.

¹³ I had fainted, unless I had believed to see the goodness of the Lord in the land of the living. ¹⁴ Wait on the Lord: be of good courage, and he shall strengthen thine heart: wait, I say, on the Lord.

ABOUT THE AUTHOR

Piper Moore is the owner and managing CEO of PM Morning in Atlanta, Georgia, where she provides results-driven professional development services, specializing in building business efficiency. She assesses the effectiveness of processes and performance behaviors while introducing business leaders to new methodologies to conquer professional challenges. In addition, she facilitates cognitive behavioral change and emotional awareness for enhanced performance through executive and personal development coaching.

With more than 20 years of experience in human resources and development under her belt, as a strategic partner to executive leaders she has assisted businesses with key functions such as succession planning, full life cycle recruiting, and establishing protocol.

Ms. Moore is a professional speaker and member of the National Speakers Association, a certified executive coach, emotional intelligence practitioner, and Franklin Covey facilitator. She has earned degrees from Miami University and Franklin University in Business Management, Business Administration, and Human Resources Management. It is her mission to help others succeed through self-awareness, empowerment, and accountability.

Ms. Moore is also the author of *New Beginnings: The journal for your journey.*

www.ingramcontent.com/pod-product-compliance
Ingram Content Group UK Ltd.
Pitfield, Milton Keynes, MK11 3LW, UK
UKHW022241230426
12048UKWH00018BA/1394